New Caribbean Junior Reader

Workbook

1

Content and skills covered in this book

Unit title	Page no. in reader	Page no. in workbook	Comprehension focus
Two Riddles	4-6	1-3	Literal, inferential
Big for Me, Little for You	7-13	4-6	Literal, deductive
Poems	14	8	Inferential
The Market	15-16	9-12	Literal, evaluative
Sports Day	17-23	14-17	Literal, deductive, evaluative
Sporting Events	24-25	18-24	Inferential, evaluative
Why the Rain Bird Calls the Rain	26-29	26-28	Inferential
Rain	30	29-31	Literal
Water Goes Round and Round	31-33	32-33	Deductive
The Wheel	34-40	35-37	Deductive, evaluative
Sending Messages	41	38	Deductive
The Morse Code	41-42	39-41	Inferential, deductive
A Light in the Old Sugar Mill	43-51	43-46	Literal, evaluative
What is a Robot?	52	47-48	Literal, evaluative
The Birthday Robot	53-59	49-51	Literal, inferential
Shoes have Tongues	60	53-55	Evaluative, deductive
The People I Know Collect Funny Things	61	56-59	Evaluative, deductive
Collecting Stamps	62	60-61	Inferential, deductive
Stamp Hunting	63-67	62-63	Deductive, evaluative
Some Interesting Animals	68-72	65-69	Deductive, literal
If I Were	73-75	70-72	Evaluative, inferential
An Aesop Fable: The Travellers and the Bear	76-78	73-75	Deductive, inferential
Old Man Moon	79	77-78	Deductive
The Moonlight Monster	79-85	79-80	Deductive, evaluative
Shadow Pictures	86	81	Literal, deductive
My Shadow	87	82	Deductive
Going to the Moon	88	83	Literal

You will find self-assessment sheets on pages 7, 13, 25, 34, 42, 52, 64, 76 and 84. These help the pupils to assess their own progress as they work through the stories and activities.

Specific skills
Locate information; select the correct answer from given answers; explore riddles; write own riddles; vocabulary; link verbal information with visual information
Locate information; explain; identify correct information; order events
Understand a text; talk about poetry
Listen and read; discuss preferences; creative writing
Locate information; give evidence from the text; discuss characters; creative writing
Identify facts; give opinions; write captions; creative writing
Explain and reason; suggest meanings; describe characters
Locate information; identify sounds; creative writing
Summarise information; correct wrong statements
Give reasons; explain behaviour; review a story
Link visual and verbal information
Answer questions; write own message in code
Match characters and actions; order events; describe characters; creative writing
Locate information; creative writing
Locate information; skim read; interpret expressions
Describe a poem; label pictures; explore rhyming words
Discuss a poem; find words with given sounds; match words with meanings; write sentences using given words
Label and match; write postcards
Answer questions; describe characters
Describe a text; odd item out; tabulate facts; write sentences; write a report
Describe a text; link information items; creative writing
Summarise; work out meanings; write a fable
Answer questions; write a poem
Summarise a story; describe characters
Describe a text; interpret visual information
Explain a poem; write own poem
Locate facts

How to use this book

To the pupil

You can work through this workbook as you read the stories, poems and other texts in your *New Caribbean Junior Reader*.

Title – This tells you which text in your *New Caribbean Junior Reader* the activity is about.

Instructions – These tell you what to do.

Questions – The questions are numbered.

Incomplete answers – Sometimes, we give you part of the answer to help you answer the question.

Answer spaces – Write your answers in the spaces provided.

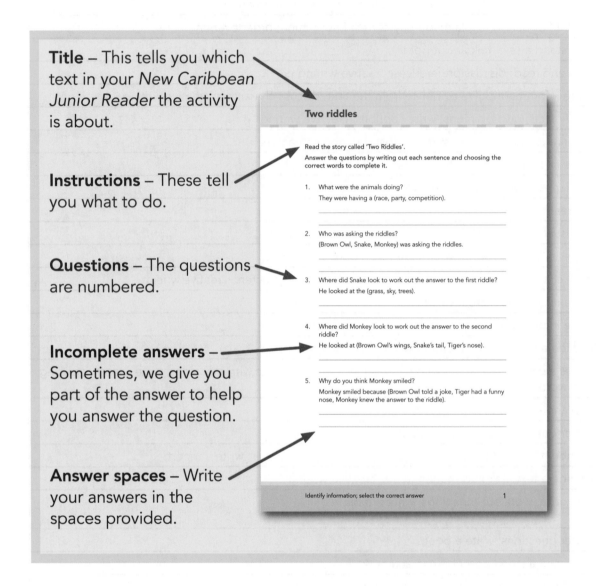

Two riddles

Read the story called 'Two Riddles'.
Answer the questions by writing out each sentence and choosing the correct words to complete it.

1. What were the animals doing?
    They were having a (race, party, competition).

2. Who was asking the riddles?
    (Brown Owl, Snake, Monkey) was asking the riddles.

3. Where did Snake look to work out the answer to the first riddle?
    He looked at the (grass, sky, trees).

4. Where did Monkey look to work out the answer to the second riddle?
    He looked at (Brown Owl's wings, Snake's tail, Tiger's nose).

5. Why do you think Monkey smiled?
    Monkey smiled because (Brown Owl told a joke, Tiger had a funny nose, Monkey knew the answer to the riddle).

Identify information; select the correct answer   1

To the teacher

This workbook is designed to be completely self-explanatory. At the back of this book, we provide information about reading and comprehension skills. The grid on the previous pages outlines the content of this workbook, shows how it relates to the reader, and explains how each unit develops pupils' reading and comprehension skills.

Two Riddles

Read the story called 'Two Riddles'.

Answer the questions by writing out each sentence and choosing the correct words to complete it.

1. What were the animals doing?

   They were having a (race, party, competition).

   _____

   _____

2. Who was asking the riddles?

   (Brown Owl, Snake, Monkey) was asking the riddles.

   _____

   _____

3. Where did Snake look to work out the answer to the first riddle?

   He looked at the (grass, sky, trees).

   _____

   _____

4. Where did Monkey look to work out the answer to the second riddle?

   He looked at (Brown Owl's wings, Snake's tail, Tiger's nose).

   _____

   _____

5. Why do you think Monkey smiled?

   Monkey smiled because (Brown Owl told a joke, Tiger had a funny nose, Monkey knew the answer to the riddle).

   _____

   _____

Follow the instructions.

6. Write out the words that appear in both riddles.

    riddle   me   ree   perhaps   two

    brothers   always   running   empty   you

    _____

    _____

7. What is a riddle? Explain in your own words.

    _____

    _____

    _____

    _____

    _____

8. Write your own riddles here. You can draw pictures as clues to your riddles.

    Riddle me riddle riddle me ree
    Guess me this riddle and perhaps not.

    _____

    _____

    _____

    Riddle me this and riddle me that
    Guess me this riddle and perhaps not.

    _____

    _____

    _____

Follow the instructions

9.   Colour the animals. Then write the correct name of each animal
     next to its picture.

| snake | brown owl | monkey | tiger | lizard | tortoise |

Big for Me, Little for You

Read the story called 'Big for Me, Little for You'.

Answer the questions by writing out each sentence and choosing the correct words to complete it.

1. What are the first words of Snake's story?

   The first words of the story are (crick-crack, slick-slack, trick-track).

   _____

   _____

2. What do all the animals shout after the first words of the story?

   They shout ("Take it back", "Break my back", "Flick-flack").

   _____

   _____

Answer in sentences.

3. Why did Snake tell the first story?

   _____

   _____

4. Which two animals was Snake's story about?

   _____

   _____

5. What did Rabbit ask Tiger to do?

   _____

   _____

6. What did Tiger say while they were fishing?

   _____

   _____

Identify information in a text

Answer in sentences.

7. Why did Rabbit get angry?

_____

_____

_____

8. Why did Rabbit let Tiger take all the big fish?

_____

_____

_____

9. What trick did Rabbit play on Tiger?

_____

_____

_____

_____

10. What lesson did Tiger learn?

_____

_____

Underline all the sentences that are correct.

Tiger played a trick on Rabbit.

Rabbit played a trick on Tiger.

Rabbit was fierce and dangerous.

When Rabbit and Tiger went fishing, Rabbit took all the big fish.

When Rabbit and Tiger went fishing, Tiger took all the little fish.

When Rabbit and Tiger went fishing, Tiger took all the big fish.

In the end, Rabbit got all the fish.

Write these sentences in the correct order.

Rabbit got very angry.

Snake said, "Crick-crack."

Tiger said, "Big for me, little for you."

All the animals said "Story end."

Rabbit played a trick on Tiger.

Snake said, "Wire bend."

All the animals shouted "Break my back."

Tiger learned a lesson.

Rabbit asked Tiger to go with him to catch fish.

Order events

Self-assessment

Put a tick in the column that best describes your work.

What I did	About the activity			
	Easy – I can do it	Quite easy but I need some help	Difficult	I can't do it yet
'Two Riddles'				
I read the story.				
I answered the questions.				
I wrote my own riddle.				
I matched the animals to their names.				
'Big for Me, Little for You'				
I read the story.				
I answered the questions.				
I chose the correct sentences.				
I put the sentences in order.				

Poems

Listen while your teacher reads the text called 'Poems'. Then follow the instructions.

1. Complete the sentence.

   This piece of writing is about _____.

2. Match up the word in the first column with the best description in the second column.

Poem	A pattern of sounds you can sometimes beat out like playing a drum
Rhythm	Short line in a poem
Verse	Something that you can look at or see
Picture	A piece of writing that might have interesting sounds and makes you imagine pictures in your mind.

3. Does the writer like poems? Yes ☐   No ☐
   How do you know?

   _____

   _____

   _____

Understand a text; talk about poetry

The Market

Read the poem aloud. Then choose the best answer to each question. Write it out.

1. What is the first line of each verse?

    a)   I like to go to the market.

    b)   I went to the market.

    c)   I went to the market with Auntie Anne.

2. Which fruit did the child and Auntie Anne see first?

    a)   They saw apples and pears.

    b)   They saw mangoes and pears.

    c)   They saw melons and pears.

3. What did the child describe as 'ripe' and 'juicy'?

    a)   The mangoes

    b)   The cabbage

    c)   The hog-plums

4. What did the child describe as 'cruel'?

    a)   The cabbage

    b)   The pigeon peas

    c)   The crabs

In the poem '**The Market**,' the child tells which foods she saw at the market, and which foods Auntie Anne bought. Follow the instructions.

1.   Complete this table.

Foods that they saw	Foods that Auntie Anne bought

Imagine that you wrote the poem. Then answer these questions.

2.   Write what you liked most and what you liked least at the market.

_____

_____

3.   What did you think about the items Auntie Anne chose to buy? Write what you would have chosen.

_____

_____

_____

_____

_____

Discussing preferences

Now write your own poem about going to the market or going shopping.

Choose another poem that you like. Write about your poem here.

Name of my favourite poem:

_____

Poet:

_____

What the poem is about:

_____

_____

_____

_____

Why I like it:

_____

_____

_____

_____

My favourite line in the poem:

_____

_____

Discussing preferences

Self-assessment

Put a tick in the column that best describes your work.

What I did	About the activity			
	Very easy	Mostly easy	Difficult	I can't do it yet
'Poems'				
I listened while my teacher read.				
I answered the questions.				
'The Market'				
I read the poem aloud.				
I chose the best answers to the questions.				
I identified the foods they saw and bought.				
I wrote about what I liked and didn't like at the market.				
I wrote my own poem.				
I wrote about another poem I like.				

Sports Day

Read the story. Complete the sentences.

1. This story is about a girl called _____.

2. Her teacher's name was _____ and her brother's name
    was _____.

3. It was _____ Day.

4. The children were _____, _____ and
    _____.

5. The only one that was not happy was _____.

6. She was _____ under the school.

7. She didn't want to take part because she could not
    _____ or _____.

8. But then her teacher asked her to help _____ some of
    the races.

9. In the end, she took part in the _____ race.

10. She placed _____ in the race.

Identify information

Say whether each sentence is true or false. Then explain how you know.

	True or false	How do you know?
The schoolchildren were very quiet.	False	They were excited, laughing and shouting.
Linda was excited about Sports Day.		
Linda's brother wanted her to take part.		
Mrs Ramchand was unkind to Linda.		
Linda didn't enjoy being a judge.		
Linda's brother was proud of her.		

Give evidence from the text

Answer in sentences.

1. What made Linda change her mind and take part in the race?

   _____

   _____

   _____

   _____

2. Who was your favourite person in the story? Say why.

   _____

   _____

   _____

3. Did you like this story? Give reasons for your answer.

   _____

   _____

   _____

   _____

   _____

   _____

   _____

   _____

Discuss characters

Write your own story about something that happened at Sports Day or while you were playing sports.

_____

_____

_____

_____

_____

_____

_____

_____

_____

_____

_____

_____

_____

_____

_____

_____

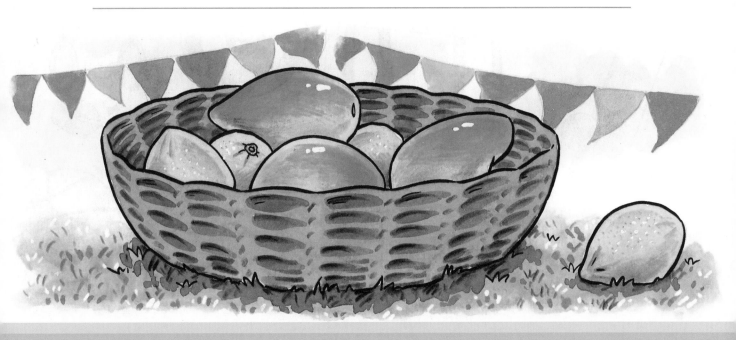

Sporting Events

Read 'Sporting Events'. For each sentence, write 'true' or 'false'. Then write the sentence from the text that helped you to work out your answer.

There is a special competition called the Crab Olympics.	
False	Of course, there is no Crab Olympics.
Only a few countries take part in the Olympic Games.	
The Olympics do not happen in the same place each time.	
The Olympics take place every ten years.	
Some athletes from the West Indies have done well at the Olympics.	
No one has heard of the West Indies cricket team.	

Identify facts

What would you say to each of these people?
Use the information from your reader in your answers.

What I would say: _____

_____

What I would say: _____

_____

Imagine that you could win a ticket to see the next Olympic Games. In order to win the ticket, you have to list ten reasons why you would like to go to the Olympics. List your reasons here.

_____

_____

_____

_____

_____

_____

_____

_____

_____

_____

_____

_____

_____

Give opinions

_____

_____

_____

_____

_____

_____

_____

_____

_____

_____

_____

_____

_____

_____

_____

_____

In newspapers and magazines, find pictures of your favourite sports stars or articles about them. Cut them out and stick them here. Next to each picture or article, write a caption. A caption is a sentence that tells us what a picture or article is about.

Write captions

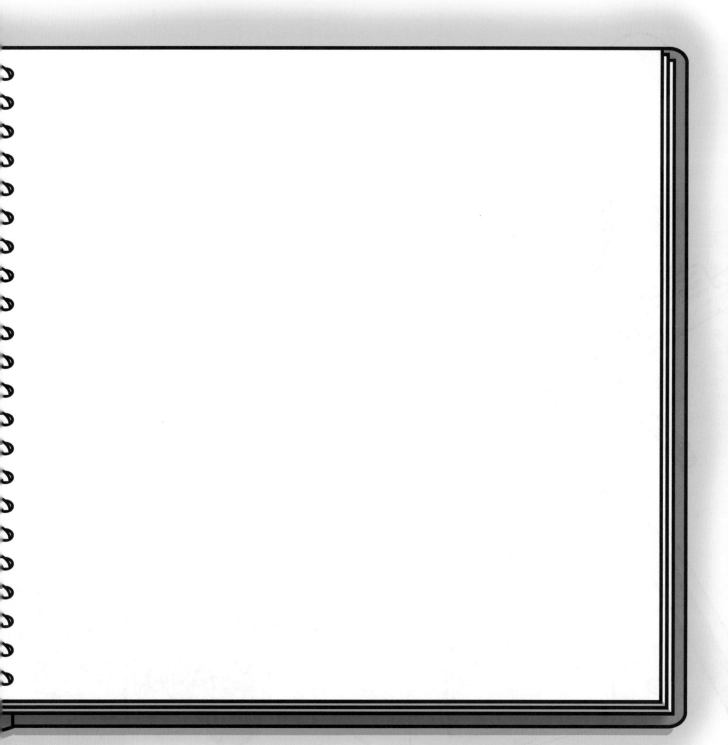

Imagine that you are a sports journalist at the Olympics. Write an interview with your favourite sports star.

_____

_____

_____

_____

_____

_____

_____

_____

_____

_____

_____

_____

_____

_____

_____

_____

_____

Self-assessment

Put a tick in the column that best describes your work.

What I did	About the activity			
	Very easy	Mostly easy	Difficult	I can't do it yet
'Sports Day'				
I read the story.				
I completed the sentences.				
I completed the 'true or false' activity and gave reasons.				
I answered the questions.				
I wrote my own story.				
'Sporting Events'				
I read the text.				
I completed the 'true or false' activity.				
I wrote my own replies to the people in the pictures.				
I gave reasons why I would like to go to the Olympics.				
I wrote captions for the pictures.				
I wrote an interview.				

Why the Rain Bird Calls the Rain

Listen to the story. Answer the questions.

1. What do you think the writer means by 'the Great Father'? Write your ideas here. Give some other names the writer could have used for 'the Great Father'.

    _____

    _____

2. What did the Great Father want the birds to do?

    _____

    _____

3. Which birds did not want to help the Great Father?

    _____

4. Why did they not want to help?

    _____

5. Do you think it is fair that they should be punished? Give reasons for your answer.

    _____

    _____

    _____

6. Did you ever have to do something you didn't want to do? Write about it and say why you didn't want to do it.

    _____

    _____

    _____

    _____

    _____

Explain and reason

Find each of these words in the story. Write in your own words what the word means. Use the story to help you work out the meanings.

Word	What it means
beautiful	good to look at
eagerly	
approaching	
lazy	
gathered	
demanded	
wonder	
hurried	
creating	
parched	

The people or animals in a story are called **characters**. Complete the table by choosing the best description for each character, and explain your choices. The first one has been done for you.

Character	Words to describe them	How do you know?
Great Father	Happy to help, hard-working, respectful of the Great Father, surprised when the cuckoos do not want to help	
Peewee	The very smallest bird	
Hummingbird	Lazy	
Cuckoos	Powerful but forgiving	He created the birds. He punished the cuckoos for their laziness, but he also forgave them afterwards.
Other birds	Very small and eager to help	

Describe characters

Rain

Read the poem 'Rain' aloud.

Complete the table by putting a ✔ next to the correct answers and a ✘ next to the incorrect ones.

Where does the writer tell us that the rain is falling?	✔ or ✘
on his head	✘
all around	
inside his house	
on the fields	
on the trees	
on the ships	
on the birds	
on umbrellas	

Listen carefully to the different sounds in the poem. Then follow the instructions.

1. Write five words from the poem that have the sound 'r'.

    _____

    _____

    _____

    _____

    _____

2. Write five words from the poem that have the sound 's', 'z' or 'sh'.

    _____

    _____

    _____

    _____

    _____

3. Write four words from the poem that have the sound 'n'.

    _____

    _____

    _____

    _____

4. Write two words from the poem that have the sound 'f' in them.

    _____

    _____

5. Think about the sounds rain makes. Write the sounds here.

    _____

    _____

Identify sounds

Now write your own poem about rain. You can use the words below to help you.

_____

_____

_____

_____

_____

_____

_____

_____

_____

_____

_____

_____

_____

_____

_____

drip   drop   splish   splash   splatter   plop   pour

rain   fall   pitter   patter   rainbow   umbrella

Water Goes Round and Round

This diagram shows the water cycle. Fill in the missing words. You can use the words in the box to help you.

Heat from the _____ makes water rise into the air.

Clouds are made up of little _____ of _____.
They are so light that they _____ in the air.

When they become bigger, they fall down as _____.

_____ falls to the ground. It collects in _____ and _____ and runs to the sea.

water   rain   sun   ponds   float   drops   rivers

Summarise information

Sally has all the wrong information! Find the correct information in your reader and rewrite each sentence with the correct information.

1. Rain comes from the sun.

    Rain comes from _____.

2. Clouds can float because they are made from air.

    Clouds can float because _____.

3. The heat from the sun makes water from rivers and ponds sink into the ground.

    The heat from the sun makes water from rivers and ponds

    _____.

4. Rivers and ponds become dry when there is a lot of rain.

    Rivers and ponds become dry when _____.

5. A cycle is something that goes in one direction and then stops.

    A cycle is _____.

Self-assessment

Put a tick in the column that best describes your work.

What I did	About the activity			
	Very easy	Mostly easy	Difficult	I can't do it yet
'Why the Rain Bird Calls the Rain'				
I listened while my teacher read.				
I answered the questions.				
I worked out the meanings of the words.				
I described the characters and explained my choices.				
'Rain'				
I read the poem aloud.				
I completed the table.				
I wrote words with different sounds.				
I wrote my own poem about rain.				
'Water goes round and round'				
I completed the water cycle.				
I corrected Sally's information.				

The Wheel

Listen to the story. Then read it on your own. Answer the following questions using sentences.

1. Why were the children excited?

   _____

   _____

2. Why was Jerry late to get onto the bus?

   _____

   _____

3. Why was Jerry thinking about the wheel of the bus?

   _____

   _____

4. The other children did not want Jerry to stop the bus. What reasons did they give for this?

Roy: _____

_____

Karla: _____

_____

Patsy: _____

_____

In a story, we sometimes discover how someone feels or what they think because of the things they do. Read 'The Wheel' carefully to help you complete the table.

Feelings and thoughts	What they did that shows us this
The children were excited.	They jumped up and down, laughed and called out to the driver.
Jerry loved buses and things on wheels.	
Roy noticed that Jerry was worried.	
Jerry's friends did not want him to stop the bus.	
Miss Jones wanted to make sure that nothing was wrong with the wheel.	
The children were interested to see the problem with the wheel.	
Mr Henry was happy that Jerry noticed the wheel.	

Explain behaviour

A book review tells us about a book: the title and author, and what the book is about. Someone that write reviews is called a reviewer. The reviewer usually gives their opinion about the book – what they liked or did not like about it.

Write a review of this story.

Story title: _____

Author: _____

The main characters: _____

The plot (what happens): _____

Why I liked (or didn't like) this story:

_____

_____

_____

_____

_____

_____

_____

_____

_____

_____

Sending messages

Read the information about 'Sending messages.'

What do you need to send these kinds of messages? Match each kind of message with the things you need.

telephone call	email	letter	poster
text message on a mobile phone	fax		

Link visual and verbal information

The Morse Code

Read 'The Morse Code' with a partner. Then answer the questions in sentences.

1. Who was the Morse Code named after?

    _____

2. Why was it named after him?

    _____

3. What two shapes do we use for Morse Code?

    _____

4. Give two different ways of sending messages in Morse Code without drawing the shapes.

    _____

5. Suggest two different situations where people might use Morse Code.

1.   Write your name using Morse Code.

_____

2.   Now write a short message in Morse Code on these two pages. Then get a friend to decode your message.

Write a message in code

Self-assessment

Put a tick in the column that best describes your work.

What I did	About the activity			
	Very easy	Mostly easy	Difficult	I can't do it yet
'The Wheel'				
I read the story on my own.				
I answered the questions.				
I completed the 'feelings and thoughts' activity.				
I wrote a review of the story.				
'Sending Messages'				
I read the information.				
I matched the kinds of messages with the pictures.				
'The Morse Code'				
I read it with a partner.				
I answered the questions.				
I wrote my name and a message in Morse Code.				

A Light in the Old Sugar Mill

Read the story. Then match each character with the correct action by drawing a line from each character's name to the action they carried out in the story.

Mr Chin	cried, 'Maa maa'.
Peter	suggested that they look for the goat.
Sarah	stopped at Mr Chin's shop on their way home from school.
The little goat	carried the bottle.
Peter	pushed some paper into the bottle as a stopper.
Sarah	asked how the goat got inside the sugar mill.
Sarah and Peter	noticed that the goat was inside the sugar mill.

Now write the sentences from page 43 in the correct order.

_____

_____

_____

_____

_____

_____

_____

_____

_____

Order events

How would you describe Peter and Sarah? For each describing word, put a ✔ for correct or a ✘ for incorrect. Then write what they did to show this.

They …	✔ or ✘	I think so because…
are helpful to their family		
are careful about safety		
care about animals		
get frightened easily		
like solving problems		
are scared of places they don't know		

When Sarah and Peter get home, they tell their mother what happened to them. Imagine this conversation. Would their mother be proud? Angry? Worried? Write the conversation between the children and their mother.

_____

_____

_____

_____

_____

_____

_____

_____

_____

_____

_____

Creative writing

What is a Robot?

Read the information about robots. Then complete the table.

Can robots...	Yes or no
Work by themselves?	
Do every kind of work better than people can do it?	
Work all day without getting tired?	
Work forever without ever breaking?	
Work in factories?	
Make motor cars?	
Learn instead of people?	

Imagine that you are a robot. Write about your life as a robot. Draw a picture of yourself.

I am a robot. My name is _____.

What I can do:

_____

_____

_____

_____

What I like about being a robot:

_____

_____

_____

_____

What I don't like about being a robot:

_____

_____

_____

A picture of me:

The Birthday Robot

First read these sentences. Then listen while your teacher reads the story. Circle the correct answers while you listen.

1. Ravi got a robot (for Christmas, for Divali, for his birthday).

2. It came from (Cameroon, Canada, Cambodia).

3. The robot had a head in the shape of a (box, balloon, ball).

4. It did not have (eyes, a nose or mouth, arms).

5. Instead of feet, it had (two wheels, two poles, two bells).

6. The lights in its eyes were (red and blue, red and yellow, orange).

7. Ravi's mother rested for a while on the (sofa, chair, bed).

8. Ravi's sister was eating (an apple, a banana, an orange).

9. In Ravi's dream, he was running away from (his father, his sister, his robot).

10. He was turning into a (robot, banana, monster).

Skimming means reading a text fast, skipping the information we do not need. Skim the story to help you fill in the missing words.

1. The robot had two things _____ _____ _____ the top of its head.

2. The robot moved _____ along.

3. "What a _____ _____ robot," Ravi said.

4. His mother screamed and sent the robot _____ off the bed.

5. His sister left the banana on the step and _____ _____.

6. His sister came back just as Ravi was _____ _____.

7. In his dream, the robot was a _____.

8. The _____ _____ were as bright as the sun.

9. His mother woke up and came _____ into the room.

10. "I am not _____," said Ravi's mother.

Write each of these sentences in a different way, using your own words. The first one has been done as an example.

1. Ravi's robot was a funny-looking thing.

    Ravi's robot looked strange.

2. "If it wasn't your birthday, you would find out something."

    _____

    _____

3. "What a great little robot!"

    _____

    _____

4. It was great fun.

    _____

    _____

5. "If you touch that banana I will tell on you."

    _____

    _____

Self-assessment

Put a tick in the column that best describes your work.

What I did	About the activity			
	Very easy	Mostly easy	Difficult	I can't do it yet
'A Light in the Old Sugar Mill'				
I read the story.				
I matched the characters with their actions.				
I described the characters and explained my choices.				
I wrote a conversation.				
'What is a Robot?'				
I read the information.				
I answered the questions.				
I wrote about being a robot.				
'The Birthday Robot'				
I listened for the answers and circled them.				
I skim read the story to find the missing words.				
I wrote sentences using my own words.				

Shoes have Tongues

Read the poem aloud.

Tick any words that describe the poem.

funny ☐   scary ☐   difficult ☐   long ☐

silly ☐   rhyming ☐   short ☐   easy ☐

Choose the correct words to complete the sentence. Circle the correct answer.

1.   This poem uses:

   a)   words that name parts of the body.

   b)   names of different countries.

   c)   nonsense words.

2.   Some words in the poem have two different meanings. The words are:

   a)   shoes, tables, chairs, needles

   b)   cannot, have, but

   c)   tongues, legs, eyes, arms

3.   The poem repeats some words. The repeated words are:

   a)   shoes, legs, eyes, talk

   b)   have, but, cannot

   c)   talk, walk, see, me

Label these pictures using words from the poem.

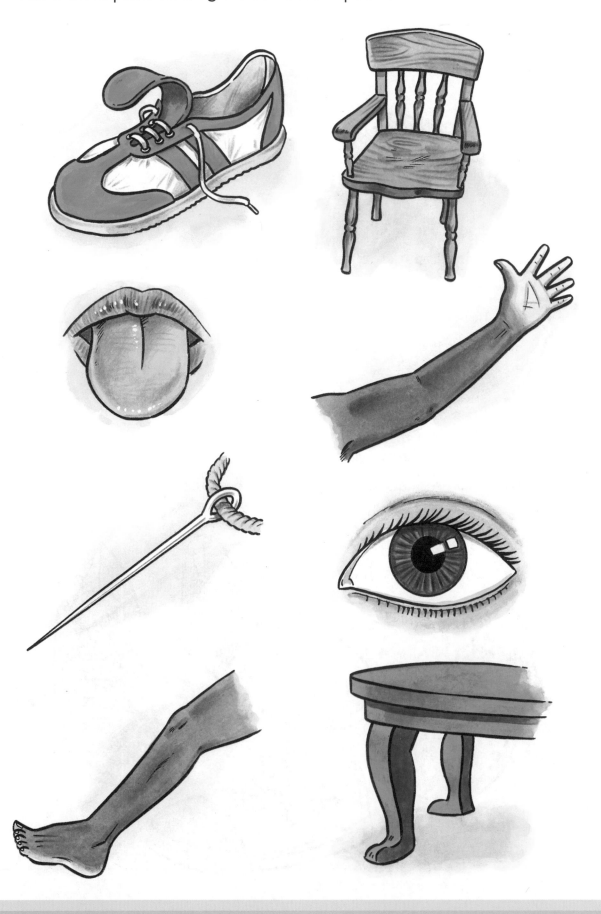

Join the words from the poem that rhyme.

| talk | see | walk | me |

Write more words that rhyme with 'talk'. Use the pictures to help you.

_____   _____   _____

Write more words that rhyme with 'see'. Use the pictures to help you.

_____   _____   _____

Now find your own words that rhyme.

_____ rhymes with _____

_____ rhymes with _____

_____ rhymes with _____

The People I Know Collect Funny Things

Read the poem aloud. Clap with the rhythm of the poem.
Tick the words that you think describe the poem.

fun ☐   serious ☐   sad ☐   silly ☐

exciting ☐   scary ☐   colourful ☐   boring ☐

Draw a line to match the characters with the things they collect on these two pages.

Circle the things that are left over. What are they?

Find words that rhyme in the poem.

things rhymes with _____

mats rhymes with_____

locks rhymes with _____

before rhymes with _____

Now find words that start with these sounds:

sh _____   _____   _____

f _____   _____   _____

_____   _____

w _____   _____   _____

p _____   _____   _____

Find these words in the poem. Match each word to the closest meaning.

Describing word	Meaning
Furry	A colour in between blue and red
Fringed	Very strange or unusual
Weird	Crazy, moving in all directions
Wild	Made out of a smooth, light (not heavy) material
Faded	Having bits of cotton or string coming out of it
Purple	Covered in fur, soft to touch
Funny	Crazy
Plastic	Odd, strange or making you laugh

Match words with meanings

Now make sentences with the describing words.

_____

_____

_____

_____

_____

_____

_____

Collecting Stamps

Read 'Collecting Stamps'.

Write the correct label under each picture.

| letter | postbox | envelope | stamp | postcard | email |

Circle the odd stamp in each set. Then say why it does not match the others.

1.

2.

3.

Imagine you are on holiday. You want to send postcards to your friends and family. Write your postcards here. Then complete the address. Draw and cut out your own stamps and stick them in the correct spaces.

Stamp Hunting

Read the story carefully on your own. Then answer using sentences.

1. What were the names of the children in this story?

   _____

   _____

2. Why couldn't the children go to dancing or play cricket?

   _____

   _____

3. What is the difference between stamp collecting and stamp hunting?

   _____

   _____

4. Why did Debbie only find one stamp at first?

   _____

   _____

5. Why didn't Debbie go into the room at the back of the house?

   _____

   _____

6. How did Debbie find the oldest stamp?

   _____

   _____

Answer questions

Describe the characters from the story. Choose a describing word from the box. Then explain why you chose it.

1.   Debbie's grandfather was _____. I think so because he

_____

_____ .

2.   Debbie's brothers and sisters were _____. I think so

because they _____

_____ .

3.   Debbie's brothers and sisters were also _____. I think so

because they _____

_____ .

4.   Debbie was _____. I think so because she _____

_____

_____ .

5.   Debbie was also _____. I think so because she _____

_____

_____ .

friendly   unfair   noisy   quiet   lucky   clever   silly   bored

Self-assessment

Put a tick in the column that best describes your work.

What I did	About the activity			
	Very easy	**Mostly easy**	**Difficult**	**I can't do it yet**
'Shoes have Tongues'				
I read the poem aloud.				
I completed the activity.				
I wrote labels and rhyming words.				
'The People I Know Collect Funny Things'				
I read the poem aloud.				
I described the poem.				
I matched items to characters.				
I found different sound words.				
I matched words to meanings.				
I wrote my own sentences.				
'Collecting Stamps'				
I read the information and completed the activity.				
I wrote postcards.				
'Stamp Hunting'				
I read the story.				
I answered the questions.				
I described the characters.				

Some Interesting Animals

Your teacher will read 'Some Interesting Animals' with you.
Tick the boxes that describe this writing.

☐ poem ☐ story ☐ information

☐ about plants ☐ about animals ☐ about people

☐ has drawings ☐ has photographs ☐ has graphs

Circle the odd one out in each set. Then say why you chose it.

bushmaster   anaconda   garden snake

_____ is the odd one out because _____

_____

_____.

iguana   crocodile   green lizard

_____ is the odd one out because _____

_____

_____.

jaguar   cat   dog

_____ is the odd one out because _____

_____

_____.

Summarise the information from the article. You do not need to use full sentences. The first one has been done for you.

Animal	Where it lives	Is it dangerous?	Size	Another fact about it
Bushmaster	Guyana, Trinidad	Yes, poisonous, kills victims quickly	Up to 5 metres	Travels in twos
Anaconda				
Iguana				
Jaguar				
Ant eater				

Find the two most interesting facts about each kind of animal from the article. Write the facts in full sentences.

anaconda

_____

_____

bushmaster

_____

_____

iguana

_____

_____

jaguar

_____

_____

ant eater

_____

_____

Brainstorm some different wild animals you would like to find out about. Complete the mind map.

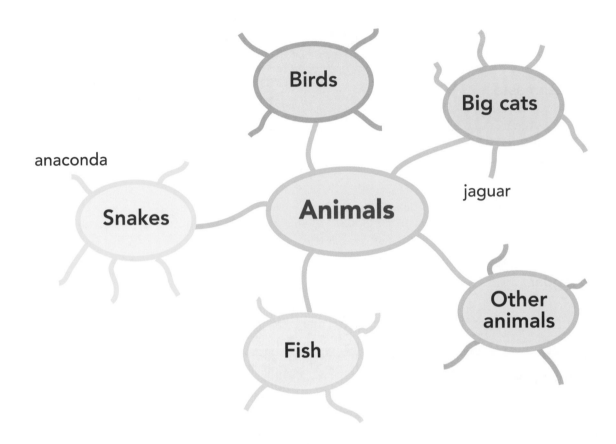

anaconda

jaguar

Now choose one of the animals. Find information in a book and use it to help you write your report on the next page.

Brainstorm animals

Another interesting animal

Name: _____

Which animal family it comes from: _____

Where it lives: _____

Size: _____

What it looks like: _____

What it eats: _____

Some other interesting facts about this animal: _____

_____

_____

_____

Why I like or don't like this animal: _____

_____

_____

_____

_____

_____

_____

_____

If I Were

Read 'If I Were' aloud. Tick the boxes that describe it.

☐ story   ☐ poem   ☐ information

☐ playful   ☐ sad   ☐ imaginative

☐ naughty   ☐ serious   ☐ scary

Choose the correct answer and then explain.

1. The person called 'I' in the poem is a

   a) mother   b) father   c) child

   I know this because

   _____

   _____

   _____

2. The person called 'I' in the poem likes to

   a) follow rules

   b) imagine herself as different animals

   c) spend time with her mother

   I know this because

   _____

   _____

   _____

Use the poem to help you find the blocks that match the heading.
Colour them the same colour. The first one has been done for you.

lizard	cricket	rat bat	earthworm
hop around	sleep	play in dirt	lie around
stick out my tongue	stay awake	suck my teeth	drag my feet
lazy	most upsetting	very naughty	chirping

Write your own 'If I Were' poem.

If I were a _____

I'd _____

And _____

In a _____ sort of way.

And my mother couldn't tell me

It's a wicked thing to do

Since she would be a _____

And she would do it too.

Now draw a picture of your poem.

The Travellers and the Bear

Read the story with a friend. Then answer the questions.

1. Suggest a different name for the story.

   _____

2. Write a summary of the story here. Your summary should say what the story is about and what happens in the story.

   _____

   _____

   _____

   _____

3. Write the meanings of these words. Use the story to help you to work out your answers.

   traveller _____

   sniff   _____

   coward   _____

Write your own fable about something that happens to two travellers.

Title _____

Once upon a time, there were two travellers. They were travelling

together. One day, they found a _____.

The first traveller said: _____

_____

_____

The second traveller said: _____

_____

_____

While they were talking, a _____ came along and

saw them.

The _____ said: _____

_____

_____

_____

_____

Then _____

_____

_____

_____

_____

The End

Draw a picture to illustrate your fable.

Self-assessment

Put a tick in the column that best describes your work.

What I did	About the activity			
	Very easy	Mostly easy	Difficult	I can't do it yet
'Some Interesting Animals'				
I listened to the information.				
I completed the activity.				
I summarised the information.				
I wrote interesting facts.				
I found information and used it to write a report.				
'If I Were'				
I read the poem aloud.				
I answered the questions.				
I matched the blocks.				
I wrote my own poem.				
'The Travellers and the Bear				
I read the story.				
I answered the questions.				
I wrote my own fable.				

Old Man Moon

Read the poem. Then answer the questions.

1. What is the poem about?

   _____

   _____

   _____

2. Suggest a different title for the poem.

   _____

3. According to the poem, why is the moon very old?

   _____

   _____

4. Why does the writer say that the moon has a birthday once a month? Is this true? Explain your answer.

   _____

   _____

   _____

   _____

5. Do you think the writer believes that this is the reason that the moon is so old? Explain your answer.

   _____

   _____

   _____

   _____

Write your own poem about the moon here. Draw a picture to go with your poem.

_____

_____

_____

_____

_____

_____

_____

_____

_____

_____

The Moonlight Monster

Your teacher will read the story aloud. Listen.
Write a summary of what happened in the story.

_____

_____

_____

_____

_____

_____

_____

_____

_____

Choose two describing words for each character. Explain your choice.

Character	Word I would use to describe them	Why
Donna		
Trevor		
Beverley		

cruel   caring   nervous   helpful   youngest

clever   teasing   creative   sorry   afraid

Describe characters

Shadow Pictures

Tick the boxes that describe 'Shadow Pictures'.

☐	story	☐	information	☐	poem
☐	instructions	☐	fable	☐	riddle
☐	only words	☐	only pictures	☐	words and pictures

Complete each column using a ✔ for correct or ✘ for incorrect.

	Bird	Alligator	Dog	Goat
Use both hands				
Use one hand				
Move the fingers				
Move the thumb				
Makes the animal's head				
Makes the animal's whole body				

My Shadow

Read the poem aloud.

1. Explain the poem in your own words.

_____

_____

_____

_____

_____

2. Write your own poem about your shadow.

_____

_____

_____

_____

_____

_____

Explain a poem; write a poem

Going to the Moon

Read the story on your own. A fact is a statement that we know is true. Use the story to help you complete the table. Write 'yes' or 'no' in the second column.

Statement	Is it a fact?
No one has ever been to the moon.	
People can travel to the moon on planes.	
People can travel to the moon in rockets.	
Space travellers take their own air with them from earth.	
Space-suits can help to protect space travellers against the hot and cold.	
There is more gravity on the earth than on the moon.	
Gravity makes things float.	
There are people called 'moon-men' on the moon.	

Self-assessment

Put a tick in the column that best describes your work.

What I did	About the activity			
	Very easy	Mostly easy	Difficult	I can't do it yet
'Old Man Moon'				
I read the poem aloud.				
I answered the questions.				
I wrote my own poem.				
'The Moonlight Monster'				
I listened to the story.				
I summarised the story.				
I described characters and explained my choices.				
'Shadow Pictures'				
I completed the activity.				
'My Shadow'				
I read the poem aloud.				
I explained the poem.				
I wrote my own poem.				
'Going to the Moon'				
I identified facts.				

About this workbook

Young children need to learn to make sense of the world around them. One of the ways that they can do this is by reading. Stories, poems and non-fiction texts which are enjoyable and informative can provide your pupils with a range of ideas and information about the world and how it works. However, in order for the pupils to benefit from their exposure to reading, they need to develop a range of comprehension skills to make sure they can work with, and understand, a range of written material.

This workbook offers practical ideas for using the *New Caribbean Junior Reader* with your class. By working through it, you can help the pupils to develop the skills they need to be able to:

- read different types of fiction and non-fiction texts, including stories, factual information reports, instructions and explanations
- identify and work with the features of readers including the contents page, sub-headings, captions, tables, diagrams and labels
- read and make sense of different kinds of diagrams, photographs and maps
- master a range of reading styles to suit the text they are working with (scan for information, read for facts, read in detail to answer a question, etc.)
- use different styles of communicating what they have read orally by explaining, retelling, arguing, reporting, discussing, selecting and debating
- select and use different styles of writing for different purposes including making notes and summaries, writing reports, letters and newspaper articles and many more.

The *New Caribbean Junior Reader* offers a range of writing in different styles – explanatory, descriptive, factual and biographical – and the authors use a range of devices in presenting the material. This makes it ideal as a basis for developing comprehension skills.

What is 'comprehension'?

The main focus of this workbook is to develop children's comprehension skills. But what do we mean when we talk about 'comprehension'? 'Comprehension' literally means 'understanding'. In order to understand a text, effective readers always ask questions about the text they are reading.

Comprehension activities train children not only to answer questions, but also to form relevant questions, in order to help them understand the information, form opinions about it, and gain insight into what they are reading.

There are four strands of comprehension skills:
- literal
- deductive
- inferential
- evaluative.

When we read, we constantly use all four of these skills – they do not occur in any particular order of importance. While we are identifying the facts presented in the text (literal comprehension), we are simultaneously linking them together to reach conclusions (deductive comprehension), bringing our own personal knowledge and experience to bear on what we are reading (inferential comprehension) and forming our opinions and judgements about the text (evaluative comprehension). Although these four strands are not discrete activities, we can distinguish between them in order to understand more fully what happens while we read.

Literal comprehension

Literal comprehension means understanding the information that the text directly presents. Literal comprehension is considered the most fundamental comprehension skill. The answers to literal questions are always 'right there in the text'. In order to develop children's literal comprehension skills, we ask them to:

- find information in a text, for example to identify the characters, places, names, dates and so on
- identify facts (answer factual questions)
- recognise 'what happened'
- order events or instructions in the correct sequence and draw time lines, flow charts and diagrams
- select appropriate information to answer literal questions, i.e. questions that ask Who? What? How many? Where? and When?

Deductive comprehension

Deductive comprehension means drawing logical conclusions from given information. A text always presents many pieces of information, but it is up to the reader to connect these pieces of information and use them to construct a meaningful whole. In order to develop children's deductive comprehension skills, we may ask them to:

- summarise paragraphs or passages
- draw pyramids or diagrams showing the main ideas of a text
- suggest titles or headings for passages of text
- explain why they think an author chose the particular language they did (e.g. words, phrases, expressive devices such as metaphors)
- provide evidence from the text to argue the author's intention or to support other conclusions
- reach their own conclusions based on explicit and implicit information
- make connections between causes and effects
- decide whether a piece of text is a fact or opinion.

Inferential comprehension

Inferential comprehension means reaching a conclusion by using our personal knowledge and experience. Inferential comprehension goes beyond the text, because the readers have to apply their own thoughts and feelings to what they are reading. In order to develop children's inferential comprehension skills, we may ask them to:

- predict what will happen next/what could happen next
- suggest the implications or consequences of actions and events
- identify with characters and their experiences, draw character profiles and character ratings
- suggest reasons for events, actions, explanations and instructions.

Some fun activities for inferential comprehension include role-playing activities and 'hot-seating' (where a pupil takes the role of a character from the text and responds to questions from other pupils).

Evaluative comprehension

Evaluative comprehension means judging how well a text suits its intended purpose and forming opinions about it. Sometimes we evaluate texts based on our personal preferences ('I liked this story/part/character because …'; 'I disliked it because …'). At other times, we appraise texts by evaluating them against a set of criteria. In order to develop children's evaluative comprehension skills, we may ask them to:

- identify the author's point of view
- say what the author wants the reader to think
- identify the effectiveness of particular aspects of the text ('How well did this part work?')
- comment on or rate the effectiveness of the whole text
- say how well the text fits its purpose, especially for non-fiction.

Some fun activities include 'Ask the author' activities, completing evaluation charts, and writing book or story reviews.

Monitoring progress

As the language teacher, you need to develop a profile of each pupil's strengths and weaknesses. The checklists which follow detail some of the most important reading and comprehension skills that primary school pupils should be developing. Use these checklists to develop your own system of assessing different pupils' abilities and to develop a record of their progress and achievement.

The skills here are progressive and are thus applicable to pupils in all grades.

Reading skills

Check that pupils are able to:

- predict what a story is about from the title and the pictures
- work out the meaning of a sentence even if they do not understand the meaning of each and every word
- use the visual cues and context to work out the meanings of unfamiliar words
- refer backwards and forwards in the text to clarify or work out the meaning of things they do not understand
- ask questions about words that are unfamiliar to them
- predict the outcome of an event based on previous reading
- read silently with understanding
- apply previously learnt reading skills to new texts
- recognise and use punctuation to read fluently with meaning.

Comprehension skills

Check that pupils are able to:

- take part in and contribute to group discussions
- add to discussions relevant to the topic
- give evidence from the extract to support their point of view
- correctly use vocabulary from the story/text in their discussion
- use the language structures of the story in their everyday speech
- talk about the story and events in it with understanding
- reconstruct the story in sequence and retell it
- draw information from the text
- understand and interpret pictures correctly
- recognise cause and effect situations.

Use the worksheets that follow on pages 89 – 92 throughout the year to encourage pupils to keep a record of what they have read and to encourage them to reflect on different pieces of writing.

My reading record

Title	Date finished	My rating
Two Riddles		☆☆☆☆
Big for Me, Little for You		☆☆☆☆
Poems		☆☆☆☆
The Market		☆☆☆☆
Sports Day		☆☆☆☆
Sporting Events		☆☆☆☆
Why the Rain Bird Calls the Rain		☆☆☆☆
Rain		☆☆☆☆
Water Goes Round and Round		☆☆☆☆
The Wheel		☆☆☆☆
Sending Messages		☆☆☆☆
The Morse Code		☆☆☆☆
A Light in the Old Sugar Mill		☆☆☆☆
What is a Robot?		☆☆☆☆
The Birthday Robot		☆☆☆☆
Shoes have Tongues		☆☆☆☆
The People I Know Collect Funny Things		☆☆☆☆
Collecting Stamps		☆☆☆☆
Stamp Hunting		☆☆☆☆
Some Interesting Animals		☆☆☆☆
If I Were		☆☆☆☆
An Aesop Fable: The Travellers and the Bear		☆☆☆☆
Old Man Moon		☆☆☆☆
The Moonlight Monster		☆☆☆☆
Shadow Pictures		☆☆☆☆
My Shadow		☆☆☆☆
Going to the Moon		☆☆☆☆

My reading month

1. Fill in the name of the month.
2. Write the name and date of each day during the month.
3. Record what you read for enjoyment each day and how long you spent reading.

Month: _____

<table>
<tr><td></td><td></td><td></td><td></td><td></td></tr>
<tr><td></td><td></td><td></td><td></td><td></td></tr>
<tr><td></td><td></td><td></td><td></td><td></td></tr>
<tr><td></td><td></td><td></td><td></td><td></td></tr>
<tr><td></td><td></td><td></td><td></td><td></td></tr>
<tr><td></td><td></td><td></td><td></td><td></td></tr>
<tr><td></td><td></td><td></td><td></td><td></td></tr>
</table>

Comprehension skills

Reading for information

Complete this form for one non-fiction book you have read.

Title: _____

Before I read this, I did not know that:

_____

_____

_____

I learned that:

_____

_____

_____

I also learned that:

_____

_____

_____

The most interesting thing in this piece of writing was:

_____

_____

_____

I'd still like to find out more about:

_____

_____

_____

I think I could find more information by:

_____

_____

_____

My book review

Complete this form for one story book you have read this year.

Title: _____

Author: _____

I found this book: easy ☐   manageable ☐   too difficult for me ☐

The part I liked most was:

_____

_____

_____

The part I liked least was:

_____

_____

_____

The most interesting thing about this book was:

_____

_____

_____

Some new words I learned are:

_____

_____

_____

If I was the author of this book I would have changed:

_____

_____

_____

Overall I would give this book _____ out of ten.

Comprehension skills